W9-CVY-111

ELEMENTARY PIANO SOLOS

soda pop
and other delights

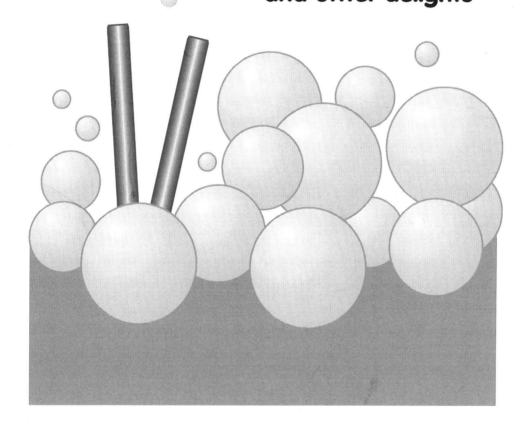

ISBN 0-88797-405-8

FREDERICK
HARRIS
MUSIC

PREFACE

These short, descriptive pieces were written for the enjoyment of children in their early years of piano study. It is hoped that the pieces will aid young pianists in the development of their technical and interpretative skills. Captions and drawings have been provided to help stimulate students' imaginations.

Linda Niamath

Original cover design by Kathy Crowe

Illustrations by Cheryl and Wendy Niamath

Contents

Can you imagine that you are gently stroking a sleepy little kitten ?

Sleepy Little Kitten

Linda Niamath

Bubbles, bubbles, bubbles, bubbles,

Up they go to the top of your pop !

Soda Pop

Linda Niamath

Quickly and brightly ♩ = 132 - 168

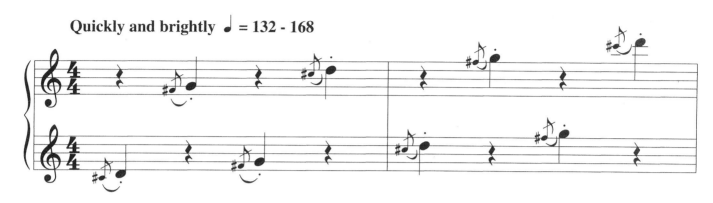

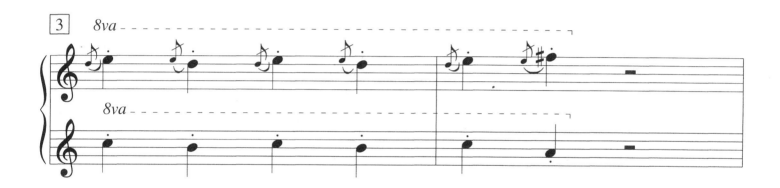

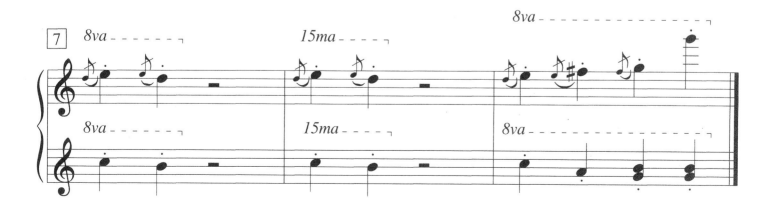

Here they come, Big Teddy showing

Little Teddy how to waltz.

Big Teddy, Little Teddy

Moderately, with warmth ♩ = 112

Linda Niamath

You are smoothly gliding over the sparkling ice,
and you'll finish with an exciting spin.

Skating

Linda Niamath

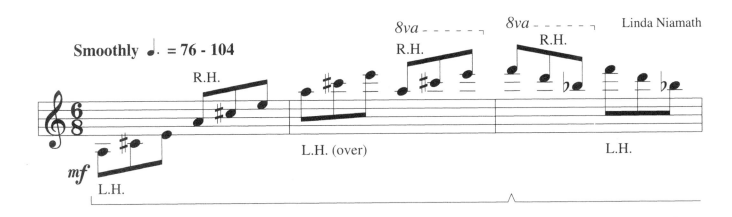

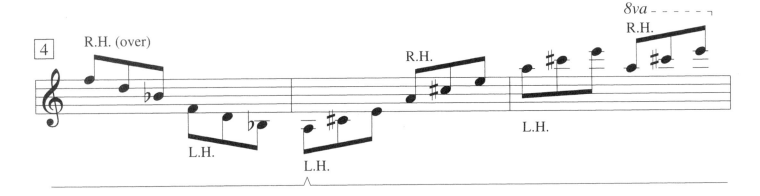

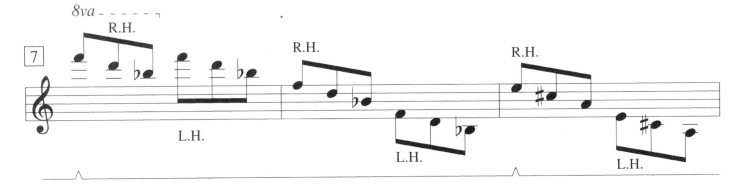

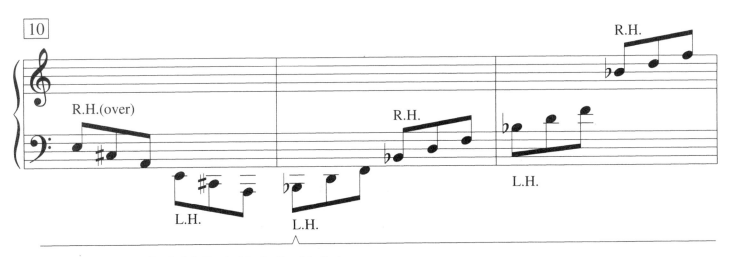

13 *accelerando e crescendo al Fine*

15

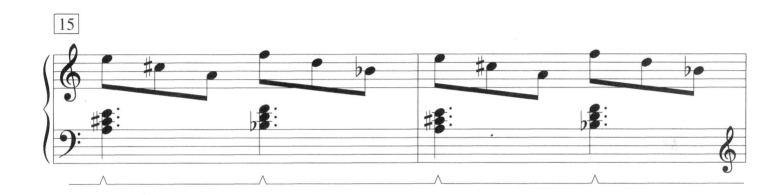

17

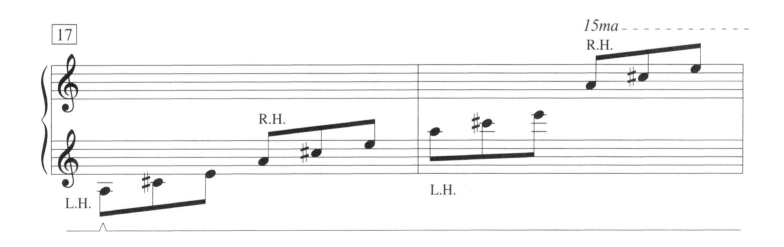

19

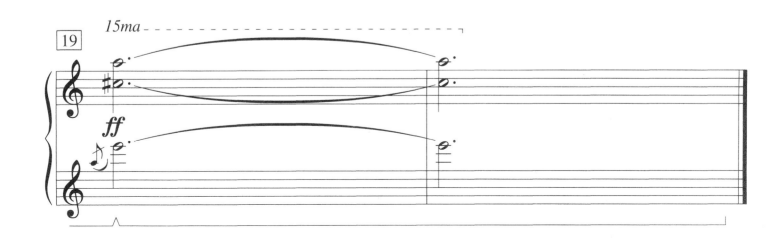

Where are you hiding —

upstairs or downstairs ?

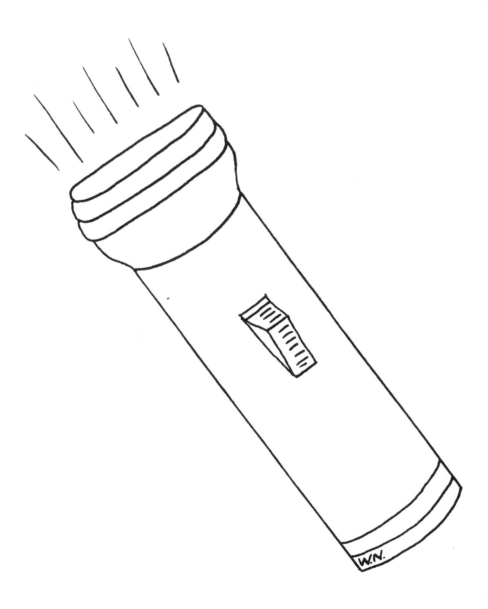

Hide and Seek

Linda Niamath

Princess — what has made you

feel so sad and lonely ?

The Lonely Princess

Linda Niamath

Wistfully ♩ = 92

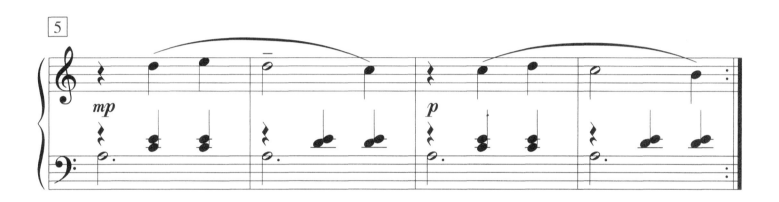

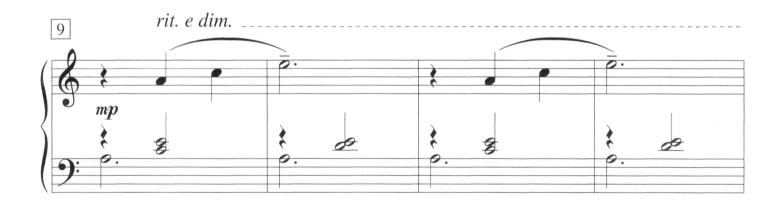

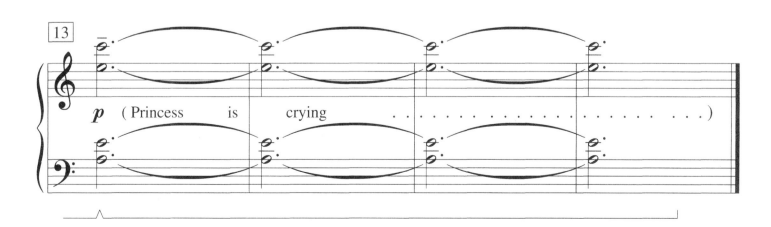

What tricks could this

little puppy be up to ?

Playful Puppy

Quickly and happily ♩ = 184

Linda Niamath

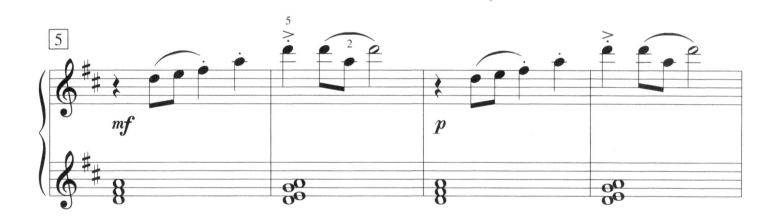

tail wagging

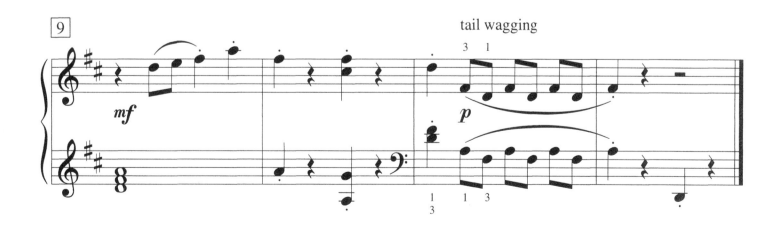

Watch out !

The Terrible Trolls are coming !

March of the Terrible Trolls

Linda Niamath

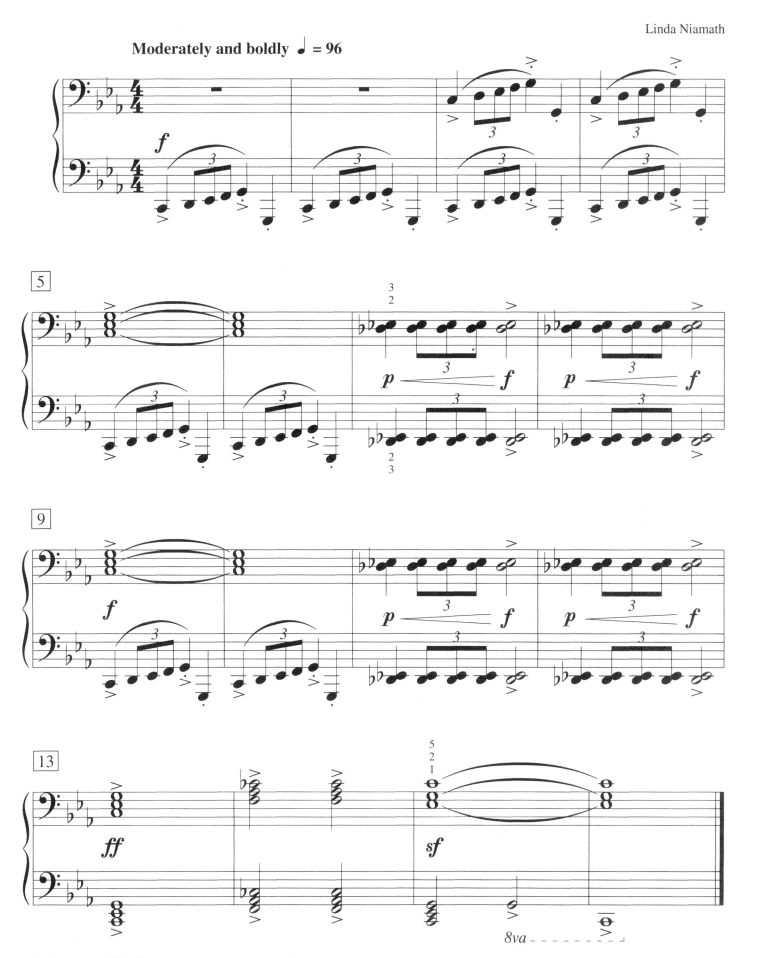

Happily swinging from branch to branch,

these little monkeys have lots of mischief in mind.

W.N.

Monkey Mischief

Linda Niamath

Quickly and playful ♩ = 152 - 168

Hurrah ! Hurrah !

It's the last day of school !

Holidays Are Here!

Linda Niamath

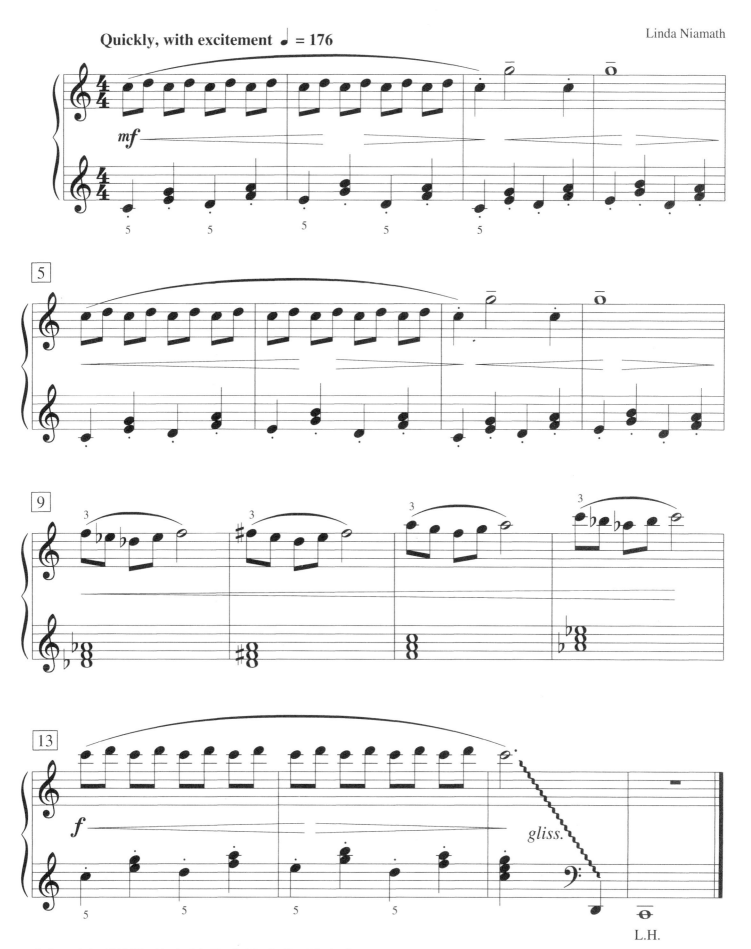

NOTES FOR TEACHERS

Considerations for each piece

1. **Sleepy Little Kitten**	phrasing syncopated pedalling
2. **Soda Pop**	grace notes
3. **Big Teddy, Little Teddy**	singing melody dotted rhythm imitation
4. **Skating**	broken triads full keyboard span syncopated pedalling accelerando
5. **Hide and Seek**	staccato contrasting dynamics shifting tonality
6. **The Lonely Princess**	expressive melody ostinato accompaniment finger independence
7. **Playful Puppy**	staccato contrasting dynamics
8. **March of the Terrible Trolls**	triplets five-finger patterns left-hand fluency
9. **Monkey Mischief**	two-note slurs five-note clusters
10. **Holidays are Here !**	trills tonal shading syncopation glissando